somewhere
between the sand
and the stardust

Volume II

somewhere
between the sand
and the stardust

Volume II

Joshua Van Leader

Copyright ©2018 JoshuaVanLeader. All rights reserved.
Published in the USA, illustrations by Joshua Van Leader.

ISBN-13: 978-1720765998

ISBN-10: 1720765995

gotong-royong

(n) [(goh-tohng roy-yuung)]

1. The joint sharing of burdens; the bearing of the weight of the world together with trusted friends

You will rise,

    beautifully

        beautifully

            beautifully.

Contents

i	100 Aspects of the moon	**12**
ii	Throughout two ends in time	**89**
iii	A quarter and a half of Stardust	**219**

Joshua Van Leader

100 Aspects of The Moon

ineffable

(adj) *[in-eff-able]*

1. Too great or extreme to be expressed or described in words.

Joshua Van Leader

She walks into a room

like the changing

of winter into spring

a change in the air,

that people adore

but only a few

will ever bring.

somewhere between the sand and the stardust II

I couldn't tell you

what was more impressive

the way the moon

lit up the night sky

or the way she looked underneath it.

Joshua Van Leader

There is an entire universe inside her and

behind those eyes, those bold, tragic eyes

are a strong woman

with whispers of inspiration

even after grief,

defying loss like it was her own shadow

still fighting through,

with a love for life like it is written

in the books I have read

it comes naturally to her

hell,

she might even

be love itself.

somewhere between the sand and the stardust II

She didn't read poetry,

what a shame

she never thought of herself as art.

Joshua Van Leader

People wait lifetimes to look at someone

the way he looks at her.

somewhere between the sand and the stardust II

So brave

to battle

her demons

everyday,

a princess of self destruction.

I will stand by her

until she sees

what I see.

The queen

I know her to be.

Joshua Van Leader

I am in two minds

caught between two worlds,

I cannot decide

if I am more

in love with your eyes

or what is behind them.

somewhere between the sand and the stardust II

In all the adventures, the events

and happenings

I have engaged in,

loving you

was by far

the most extraordinary,

abstract,

ecstatic adventure of them all.

She spoke with softness yet decisiveness:
"If you fall in love with me. You will fall in love with my favourite movie scripts and song lyrics and the stars and the long summer evenings ahead. The essence in comfort of winter days. You will be enchanted so naturally and so freely that it may be hard, if ever, to find a love like mine again. Because if you fall in love with me there will be no doubt, that I will love you the way no one ever has. I will of invested so much into you there will be no speculation of anything to come.
You will never know a love like it.

    I am that kind of person."

somewhere between the sand and the stardust II

I can't explain

why I am so in love with you.

Maybe it is that no ones else

makes me feel so alive inside

or maybe the way you take

me to another place,

that no one else ever has

and no one ever can.

Joshua Van Leader

Give me a night sky filled

with lights from

other worlds

let me drink in the idea

that one day;

they will guide me to you again.

somewhere between the sand and the stardust II

Hazelnut eyes and a heart

as fierce as the seas

with a mind

as wild

as it

was free

a walking eulogy

from all the

corners of astrology.

Joshua Van Leader

It is not until

you have been broken by love

that you then know

how strong you really are.

All the poems in the world

but not one enough to fulfil you.

Joshua Van Leader

Just in that moment

she looked at me

although

it was silent

her eyes spoke,

roaring with emotional fires,

I felt the echo of love through my veins

speaking was unbearable

the words I had to say

were futile,

the suspense built

so I stayed

stranded and vulnerable

warranting her eyes to go on

and destroy me.

somewhere between the sand and the stardust II

He wasn't always like that,

he did love once.

But he was broken by love.

How do you expect someone

who loved loving and trusted it

in its purest form,

    to ever love again?

She is a waterfall,

of opulence and confidence.

A fountain of kindness,

a cascade of peace.

What was truly admirable and irresistible

about her; was that she was a *well*.

A *well* of knowledge and creativity,

with compassion and affection at the bottom,

plunging into the depths of her

you will only find more and more that

interests and fascinates you.

You can't know her by just looking at her,

not from the surface.

You have to wait and be composed

to discover her gifts and secrets.

Her *well* of love is not easily given.

Joshua Van Leader

You underestimated them

and that was your greatest flaw.

You will forever look at a fire

and only ever see a flame.

somewhere between the sand and the stardust II

Nobody is to blame for what happened.

I am not angry with you.

I have put out that flame and the ashes have

blown with the wind.

I went through many moments where I tasted

salt in every mirror I looked into.

After hating what surrounded me

and equally; hating myself.

It was a viscous cycle

thirsty for self neglect

with no meaning of how you made me fall

into this revolution.

I will carry these scars internally

they will remind me that I am

my own conquerer

my own hero

my own victor.

Joshua Van Leader

>
> I will not question
>
> the heavens in her eye,
>
> I see them
>
> even if she doesn't,
>
> the mirror
>
> we all know,
>
> it can lie.

somewhere between the sand and the stardust II

Life is a little too short

to do the same thing

repeatedly

the only thing

that should be consistent

    is who you love.

Joshua Van Leader

I'm not sure where she came from

she stays up late at night

talking to the seas of stars,

about something hands cannot write

she talks in riddles of how

she will never need a knight

under the moon you see why,

too strong to control,

too bold, too bright.

somewhere between the sand and the stardust II

It is the mind that needs to breathe,

too much thinking

will always drown the heart.

Joshua Van Leader

I remember now,

the worst parts of me

showed all

the darkest fragments

of how you made me feel.

I ask myself

now

how did I get so addicted

to where you made me kneel?

somewhere between the sand and the stardust II

> Her beauty
>
> is not solely something you can see.
>
> Her true beauty
>
> lies in having the privilege
>
> to what the eyes cannot see.

Joshua Van Leader

It was dinner,

a small boutique restaurant.

A summer evening and her heartbeat rose

like wildfires alongside her mind raced

questioning:

Was it all real? All this effortless romance?

Then it struck her, she knew in faith.

All the stories she had read,

the lyrics she had heard,

they were real,

she wasn't afraid to tell herself

this is it,

this adventure of love.

It starts now

loving him,

truly may never end.

somewhere between the sand and the stardust II

When it rains on her

it is not grey.

It is always full of colours

that have been dying

to touch her skin

vibrated from the stars,

pulsated through the clouds.

Joshua Van Leader

Anyone,

who ever loved

dies a poet.

somewhere between the sand and the stardust II

She bled in hues of blue

it looked like oceans of sapphire ink

were being streamed gently from inside her.

Vast oceans of imagination emerged,

with constellations of love,

peace vibrating through her fingers,

if she ever felt like touching you

you would feel it

for you would burn with euphoria.

Joshua Van Leader

somewhere between the sand and the stardust II

I'm sure of it.

Her life was a wondrous living eulogy

the stars would always

kiss her skin,

the sun

arose every morning

just to see her

go do her magic.

Joshua Van Leader

The heart bled.
The stars listened.
The ocean healed.
The soul forgave.

somewhere between the sand and the stardust II

It went pitch black,

there was silence

and then there was a crack of lighting

sounding like a

bolting through stone.

I knew then

it was heartbreak,

it was never going to be easy to

come back after that.

But you did.

You did.

Joshua Van Leader

She was not as wealthy as them

but she was always

richer in taste.

He implored:

    "You can't hide your heart forever."

She uttered:

    "It's not hiding, it's flying around somewhere else, we are too focused on loving other things in life sometimes that come only in halves. I'm certainly not going to waste and worry it away on a half measured charm like yours."

Joshua Van Leader

She walks with a gold painted heart

madly free and clear in her mind

so determined.

She is everything she wanted to become,

powerful in her actions,

dignified in her principles.

She breathes with an essence

of integrity that other women admire,

a courage others aspire to carry.

Just don't be too careful.

Only if she cares to,

she may look at you

she will freeze you.

Yet at the same time,

melt you to the ground.

It wasn't what she created.

It was how she created.

It wasn't what she bought.

It was always how she wore it.

It was always how she lived;

that was timeless

for she was

consistently, unpredictably, superfluous.

Joshua Van Leader

She has integrity and decency

elegance calls her

and kindness follows her

she has things you can't buy

but you will inevitably

pay to get closer to.

somewhere between the sand and the stardust II

        Well if it isn't her heart

     that makes you see colour

       then it will be her mind

      you have no choice but

          to see everything

     when you are with her.

Joshua Van Leader

I have seen many

beautiful things in my life

but the garden of her soul,

the thoughts behind those eyes

is beauty that cannot be reached.

somewhere between the sand and the stardust II

It was by accident

that your hand touched mine

but it sent a pulse

I have not felt before,

the blue blood in my veins

spiralled and churned

I swear it exploded

something inside me

and for that moment

my insides turned gold.

Joshua Van Leader

She was the only poetry,

anyone ever needed.

somewhere between the sand and the stardust II

He adorns you,

he really does admire you,

I have only ever seen a love like that

and it was between the stars and the sky.

I have never seen

a love like that between two people.

Joshua Van Leader

She fell in love with poetry,

with characters she studied,

the moonlight and its reflection,

with an understanding that

to most she was too abstract.

She mostly didn't care,

she wasn't going to settle

for someone who made her feel ordinary,

she wanted something on fire,

something unusual

something out of this world.

somewhere between the sand and the stardust II

        She had eyes

    that made oceans move,

     oceans of stardust.

Joshua Van Leader

Her skin was kissed by flowers

and her words were seeds to my soul.

somewhere between the sand and the stardust II

She sits on the cliffs

and looks out at sea

she soaks it all in

at all she can be,

as the hues of the blues

from the seas to the skies,

empty their hearts

and fill up her eyes.

Joshua Van Leader

Her eyes had colour

that even rainbows

had never seen

but her heart,

that was painted

in the same bright light of the stars.

somewhere between the sand and the stardust II

I think she wanted

a love that felt safe

and then something fierce

when it needed to be.

Joshua Van Leader

You are only as beautiful

as how you make someone else feel.

somewhere between the sand and the stardust II

At first they would natter

how strange

and different

she was

but they never noticed

eventually,

they were only copying her.

Joshua Van Leader

Her eyes

so blue,

calming,

and still crawling with spirit

looking into them

long enough

you will feel like you are swimming.

somewhere between the sand and the stardust II

Hurricanes of emotions

swirled in her heart,

with typhoons of ideas

floating through her art

and cyclones of stardust

ran through her blood,

she was all the oceans together

though often,

misunderstood.

Joshua Van Leader

She was rare and peculiar,

she was foreign but familiar.

somewhere between the sand and the stardust II

Be careful when you love her,

she may scorn you unintentionally

she is made of oceans,

oceans of fire.

Like champagne;

romance,

is just an elegant extra.

somewhere between the sand and the stardust II

I found myself thinking

about you

and then naturally

I found myself thinking about love.

Joshua Van Leader

I felt my heart explode

shattering,

into a million stars across a galaxy

I always thought unreachable

with the weight of an affection

that anchored me, I was drenched

in your love but it felt

like home with the stars

so happy to be free,

with a belief and conviction,

that this was the love

my soul had waited for.

All this time.

You.

somewhere between the sand and the stardust II

The best piece

of music

I have

ever heard

was that

of my own doing.

It was

the beating

of my heart

synchronising

onward

to the strings

of my mind

from when

I first

met you.

Joshua Van Leader

She was not easily defeated.

Taking on trials

executing them decisively.

Caught reading

and sitting amongst the flowers

watching nature nurture,

she was often in a tranquil state

but she had been hurt before,

deceived and lied to.

However, she never blamed anyone else,

no, she wore her mistakes and scars proudly

she knew that the past

always came to an end

somewhere between the sand and the stardust II

so she continued to travel

watching others fall into great loves

and never envied them,

observed the stars,

grew with self belief,

repeatedly conquered her demons,

lived on a beautiful tale

and her love for others

was a reflection

of how beautiful her life was lived.

Joshua Van Leader

She is bodacious,

a living intoxication.

somewhere between the sand and the stardust II

She lived a life of poetry

and she knew that

because people didn't understand her

they feared her or envied her

only to an extent, nevertheless

it is all the same to her

she embraced a different way of thinking

and with that,

inspired courage and imagination,

innovation and originality

she was without doubt

a truly

majestic woman of time

and that is being reserved.

Joshua Van Leader

If only you could see

the gold from your spirit

to your fingertips

how I hope

that one day,

you will catch a glimpse of

how it feels to look at you.

somewhere between the sand and the stardust II

She absorbed

all the patience

from the woods

and applied it to her spirit

she took the wisdom from the stars

and applied it to her mind,

she took the power of the sun

and put it forward in her actions

she took the fierce nature of the sea

and she applied it forthright

into everything

she wanted to be.

Joshua Van Leader

There is something incredibly

soothing and beautiful about a storm

maybe it is that you know it will pass

or that you find comfort in knowing

even nature also looses control

and must express its anguish

or maybe

it is that you see beautiful things

where most people see chaos.

somewhere between the sand and the stardust II

She is some kind of perfect.

A perfect I have never tasted before.

Joshua Van Leader

Your heart will ache

for a little while

and your mind

will tell you

to never love again

but that would surely mean defeat,

take this day by day,

through seasons it will take,

but you will not break,

not today, not tomorrow, not ever.

somewhere between the sand and the stardust II

You will *Always* return brighter than the fire,

you will *Always* prove

to be more powerful than the storm,

you will *Always* shine through the darkness

and you will *Always* defeat the shadows,

Always

Always

Always.

Joshua Van Leader

She has ethereal eyes

look into her

you'll see kaleidoscope skies.

somewhere between the sand and the stardust II

She was darkness to many

but to me

she was darkness that brought mystery

like the night

she would rhyme with the stars

dance with the moon

she was the romantic enigma

everyone searched for,

she was dark in parts, yes.

One to be more admired,

than ever feared.

Joshua Van Leader

She always believed in true love.

That it will one day find her.

So much,

that she lived

for herself

by herself,

for many years,

sharing love

where she went with family and friends,

creating, growing, learning,

until, she found

the best and foremost love

came from within.

somewhere between the sand and the stardust II

Look into her eyes long enough

and I swear

you will see galaxies and stars and universes

you may never be the same again.

Joshua Van Leader

She was brave enough to love once.

She breathes

locking in the courage to love again

it is time to love herself

for a little while

the days are hers

to paint the sky whatever colour she wants.

somewhere between the sand and the stardust II

The Between

Throughout

two

ends

in

time

Joshua Van Leader

aesthete

(adj)

1. Someone with deep sensitivity to the beauty of art or nature.

Joshua Van Leader

The man who runs his own mouth

will always end up drowning in his own words.

somewhere between the sand and the stardust II

Live with more passion

about the way you do things,

with an impenetrable, moving heart

a plausible, strong character

and a way to make the

unthinkable, thinkable.

Joshua Van Leader

What if your skin was peeled back

and you were inside out

heart exposed,

your rawness and true self shows.

Would you still be beautiful then?

When you force

something that is

supposed to contain feeling

you will never attain

its true purpose.

Joshua Van Leader

You will find the space

in your heart to love fiercely again

the void that spaces your mind and heart

will draw to a close once more

the skies will rain

stardust on your soul

whilst thriving and

dancing among the stars

burning brighter than ever before

the magic inside you will feel at home again.

somewhere between the sand and the stardust II

Joshua Van Leader

a poem a day,
keeps the demons away.

ataraxia

(n) *[at-uh-rak-see-uh]*

1. A state of freedom from emotional disturbance and anxiety; tranquillity

Joshua Van Leader

Write your own story

let the pages bleed with emotion

let the chapters compel you to continue,

let your book burn through the skies.

somewhere between the sand and the stardust II

> Do not be easily tempted by beauty
>
> its contribution is as temporary
>
> as it appears to be.

Joshua Van Leader

I dream of a world

far different from this

my soul

constantly searches

for something more

something further

than the stars we see

my mind is here

but my soul is from another place.

somewhere between the sand and the stardust II

Just as the stars

go on

                                          and on

                   and on

as will you.

Joshua Van Leader

I don't believe

in many *'forevers'*.

I've heard them spoken often

and used a little too easily

but I know of my forever

and that it will last this lifetime at least

once it is promised

it will be proven

through the way

I love you everyday

not by any words

I could ever

simply say.

somewhere between the sand and the stardust II

Throw yourself into the sky

ricochet between dreaming and reality,

absorb everything

let your soul feel nothing

or maybe feel everything

even if only,

for a little while.

Joshua Van Leader

somewhere between the sand and the stardust II

Create

because there is a part

of who you truly are

that will not be still.

Write

because the voices in your head

will not stay quiet.

Love

because that is the only thing that

is ever worth doing.

Joshua Van Leader

Be thankful

for overthinking

because not everyone

has that intelligence to do so.

IF IT WAS EASY

THEN EVERYONE ELSE

WOULD ALREADY

BE DOING IT.

KEEP GOING.

Joshua Van Leader

The mirror lies

it shows only

what you want

the world to see

it isn't true, it isn't you

you are not what it depicts.

You are Beautiful

somewhere between the sand and the stardust II

The stars and the moon

are evidence

that the truest beauty,

can always be found

throughout the long stretches of the darkness.

Joshua Van Leader

Remember

it is about the story

it is never about being *happy* throughout it all.

It is about looking back at the end

and saying;

"What a hell or a ride."

somewhere between the sand and the stardust II

Your problems

are only seeds to grow yourself.

Joshua Van Leader

A library is a forest of knowledge.

A bookshop is a sea of broken hearts.

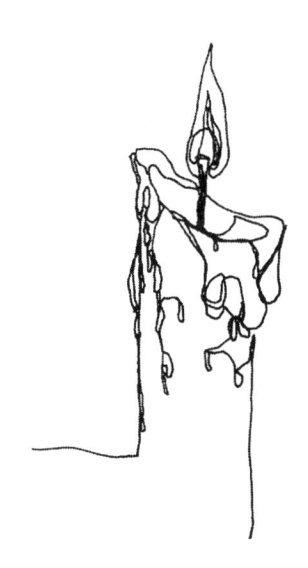

Your light in someones life

is your art.

your light is your art,

your light is your art,

your light is your art.

Joshua Van Leader

Even if all you can do is sit in your room

with nothing but your thoughts

then that's what you have to do

for a little while,

too much of everything ain't no good

too much of nothing ain't good either.

Find a balance

and allow yourself grace

then give yourself time to grow.

If the world is going somewhere

then you're going with it.

somewhere between the sand and the stardust II

I'd really enjoy to talk about my dreams,

what I envision and see everyday.

But I'm too busy dreaming

and too busy living in them.

Joshua Van Leader

Make sure to get that alone time in,

get to know yourself

treat yourself as *easy* as it appears.

Build up that confidence within you.

Remember and keep remembering

that you control everything around you;

the people, the places,

even your choice of coffee.

This is your life, your liberty, you must

embrace the comet you are, the stardust built

in you is just waiting to always be used,

you don't need to prove anything to anyone,

you are the sparks of the flame from the sun.

Just consider yourself an instinct itself

and live on that instinct.

Meraki -

Embrace the brokenness,

put the fragments of your

new self back together

in a different way than before

let people figure it out eventually

that you are not the same.

You are a new kind of flame.

Joshua Van Leader

At times

we all need to be left alone

to breathe,

to be grateful perhaps

or just to sit and wander

into the sea of stars.

somewhere between the sand and the stardust II

Allow yourself the time you need to heal

and recover thoroughly

there is no medicine for a broken heart

or a punctured mind.

Give yourself grace

and get to know yourself

through it all a little better.

It is an opportunity,

it is an opportunity

for so many, many beautiful things to come.

Joshua Van Leader

'Light Giving' -

Don't be distracted

about others dreams and others stories

take comfort

in your own dreams

and make your own stories.

Self enlightenment is invaluable

for there is so much light inside you

even when

you do not see

or feel it

there is a fire

that you may not feel

but it is there.

Joshua Van Leader

>You knew me
>
>in just a chapter
>
>of my life
>
>where I was still searching for my
>
>true self
>
>how can you say
>
>you know me?

somewhere between the sand and the stardust II

Remain content

with what you currently have,

while striving

for what you want

in patience and in a diligent silence.

Joshua Van Leader

If you create something unique or innovative

expect to get questioned, expect negativity,

expect nothing great at first.

Continue to strive towards the ideal

that is in your head,

because it is your vision and

you can, you can do this.

I WOULD LIKE TO
UNSUBSCRIBE FROM
YOUR BULLSHIT.
PLEASE NO LONGER
INCLUDE ME IN
ANYTHING AT ALL
TO DO WITH YOU.

THANK YOU.

Joshua Van Leader

I am with you

but I will not do it for you.

I am not in your mind

but you are in there somewhere.

I can not see stardust.

But I sure as hell know you breath it,

because I can feel it,

whenever I am near you,

I feel that magic.

And what now then?

Well,

you pick yourself up from the dirt

and you go again.

It will be a regular act throughout life.

Because that is a life worth living.

Joshua Van Leader

I'm knackered.

Me too

and I've only lifted up

a couple glasses of wine.

somewhere between the sand and the stardust II

I'd rather

go out

like a true,

comet on fire

than

a rotting,

mouldy apple.

Joshua Van Leader

You deserve to feel

like you are among the stars,

like you are sitting on the moon.

somewhere between the sand and the stardust II

The only important thing to live by is:

'Make beautiful moments.'

Joshua Van Leader

Don't drown in love,

don't become blind.

You shouldn't lose yourself

whilst finding someone

you want to spend the rest of your life with.

Joshua Van Leader

Your art

can be as simple

as loving another

emphatically.

somewhere between the sand and the stardust II

Depression -

You were meant to admire the rain

you were not meant to sit in it.

Joshua Van Leader

I'm not really interested
in anything normal.
Normality is something that
brings out bad habits for me,
it is a little boring too,
it tastes stale
and to be honest,
I want my soul to be on fire,
I want my fingertips to burn
with creativity and love for
what I do
normal never has been
and never will be for me.

When you suffer from depression

you don't feel 'sad'.

Actually,

you don't feel anything at all,

finding ones self worth

drowned in self doubt

but you are not alone,

you do not have to suffer in silence,

take your thoughts,

and throw them into the skies

scream into the seas let it all go in whatever

way you find riveting. Look to encourage

your mind, give it time to heal, to

trust again, to progress, to love everything

anew, but more importantly,

love you too.

Joshua Van Leader

There are the broken skies

with rains that bring thunder

then the unhinged oceans

that drown us all in wonder

with cyclones and typhoons and hurricanes

but all they ever do

is remind you to be you

and that all the broken pieces

will always shine on through.

somewhere between the sand and the stardust II

My heart felt heavy

and sometimes

just sometimes

sometimes I spoke in riddles.

Joshua Van Leader

somewhere between the sand and the stardust II

If it doesn't test my character

or make my soul dance,

my mind wander

along the margins of what we know

my heart pound

in an exhilarating and stimulating beat

then I'm not at all interested

in what it is.

Joshua Van Leader

You learn from your lessons

you learn to respect them,

show appreciation towards such things

because they are a part of you

they too,

had a purpose for you.

somewhere between the sand and the stardust II

I have lived many romances

many beautiful,

alluring romantic moments

that were all just in my head.

Joshua Van Leader

If you don't believe in magic

how can you emphasise

so much belief in love?

somewhere between the sand and the stardust II

If it does not

make you feel like a better person

then simply, forgive it

then

let it go.

Joshua Van Leader

You are not built to withstand pain

or to fight against it permanently,

the best way to deal with pain

is to accept

that it will continue to come

across your life,

that it deserves

a formidable respect

but that is all.

somewhere between the sand and the stardust II

We get a little caught up

in search for a happiness in life

we are creatures inside a cage here,

specs of stardust

amongst a vast universe

give that some thought

and enjoy the process of life.

Joshua Van Leader

There is no shame

in admitting depression

there can only be a relief

from having such courage

to admit that your mind wanders,

your troubles get a little much

its simply;

just pure bravery.

somewhere between the sand and the stardust II

You may have many faults

as many of us are far from perfect

but tricking someone into love

should never be one of them.

Joshua Van Leader

**CREATE ART
WHATEVER IT MAY BE
THAT PAINS YOU,
EXCITES YOU
OR EVEN
SCARES YOU**

TURN IT INTO ART

somewhere between the sand and the stardust II

Joshua Van Leader

My mind longs for some alternative.

Romances fabricated in my world

of imagination,

my heart loathes in loneliness

I feel everything at once,

inside I feel trapped

and so

on the outside,

I burn,

burn burn with creativity.

somewhere between the sand and the stardust II

It is important to observe

to nurture and reflect on everything

but keep telling your instinct to grow

for the garden of life

is meant to be a little wild.

Joshua Van Leader

In order

to be

loved and respected

for what you do

you must

be willing

to be hated

for it too.

somewhere between the sand and the stardust II

There is beauty in chaos

but deceivingly

there too;

is chaos in beauty.

Joshua Van Leader

Have an

imagination

that will stretch out

the night sky

and a love

that would

fill it.

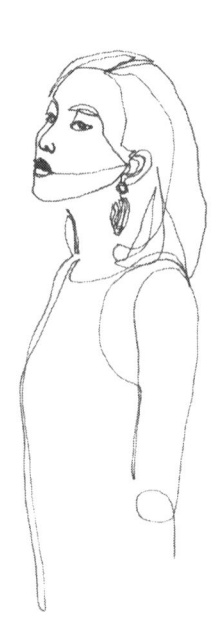

somewhere between the sand and the stardust II

For every love lost

there is a love gained,

that is the balance.

Joshua Van Leader

If you must ever

question your self worth

to do anything in life

then remember

there is always another option.

somewhere between the sand and the stardust II

Try rising with the sun

and filling out your days

with actions

that make you feel on fire

that stretch

the strings

of your heart

and connect

the wondrous avenues

of your mind

together.

Remember,

you are

just a comet passing through.

Joshua Van Leader

Our fears

are parallel

to our

problems

what we fear

is often

just our

imagination drowning.

somewhere between the sand and the stardust II

In order to be great at something

you must be willing

to be crap at it first.

There is much to be said

for being busy

with your own thoughts,

just because you are alone

does not mean you are lonely.

You hold avalanches of ideas,

you carry a rich mind

that should be manifested frequently,

cultivating new ideas and developments

are what stems your life,

be comfortable

with sitting within the wild

Neverland of your own self

and get a little lost there for a while.

somewhere between the sand and the stardust II

People

don't mind

their own business

because

their own

business is boring.

Joshua Van Leader

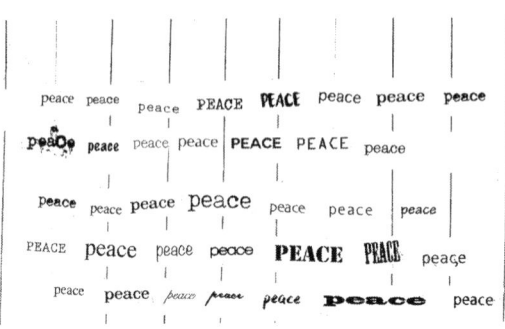

peace peace peace PEACE PEACE peace peace peace
peace peace peace PEACE PEACE peace
peace peace peace peace peace peace
PEACE peace peace peace PEACE PEACE peace
peace peace peace peace peace peace

If you see everything

as art

you admire it more.

It is an ongoing, further study in life.

You develop a sense of deeper gratitude

that the universe falls in love with,

for art is the universes favourite entity.

Joshua Van Leader

It is ok

to go back to your past.

The summers where you spent growing up

where you had your first kiss,

it is ok to revisit

the past that has left scars on you

remember that these events

shaped you into who you are today

and without any of that

good or bad

you wouldn't have a tomorrow.

somewhere between the sand and the stardust II

Everyone has their own fight,

their own battle

everybody faces something,

that worries them.

Joshua Van Leader

It is just life.

I wrote and I created

my way out of the hell,

the chaos

in my mind

but every so often

it leans in and whispers

fall into me again,

oblivion.

somewhere between the sand and the stardust II

The void called out your name again

and again I replied:

"I let them go, long ago

steer away, go and conduct to their greedy

eyes, they are nothing but shadows

and grey clouds to me now,

do not bother me

with such thoughts in summer."

Joshua Van Leader

I like to sit

with the window open

even if the rain is hammering

and exhausting itself

with the wind

drowning

in its own echo.

I find comfort

in knowing

that they too

want to be heard and felt

that even nature

needs to explode and break sometimes.

somewhere between the sand and the stardust II

It scorched my perspective,

you really did break me, you know?

The sky bled,

where most people see blue skies

I saw red and black.

Joshua Van Leader

Your kingdom

is just that.

It is yours,

don't you forget that

no one else

gets to rule it

and you should

feel nothing but gratitude

from those who

get to be a part of such a wonder.

somewhere between the sand and the stardust II

I could of

thought

of anyone,

any place, anytime, anywhere,

and I thought of you.

The truth is,

I always have,

and I always will,

because always is always

even when we're old or ill,

again,

always is always,

always until forever stands still.

Joshua Van Leader

Old flames

tend to try and come back

and set a light

to everything you have tried to rebuild

very rarely

do they return

to provide more comfort and solidify trust,

they return

to burn your entire house down again,

don't allow an old flame to spark.

Blow it out

and move the hell on.

somewhere between the sand and the stardust II

I find the warmest of blues

in the greyest of skies

I see oceans of stars

within your heavy, melancholy eyes.

Joshua Van Leader

The way you fall asleep, the way you walk,

the way you make your coffee,

the way you drink your coffee.

How you speak and treat another,

the way in which you read, how you write,

the way you watch the stars, it's all art.

Don't you understand, the way you look at the

world is art, the way you are seen is art.

everything we know to exist; is art.

Hiding from your fear

only gives it more strength,

and more purpose to destroy you.

Joshua Van Leader

It was when I felt that I had lost everything

that in truth

I found,

I had everything I ever needed.

It is important to experiment in life

to love wildly but honestly

create dangerously and endlessly

to your hearts content with integrity,

to go through life roaring and fighting with

a stride of discipline yet to not forget

to do it all with no expectations,

for that will allow you grace and give you a

better chance of enjoying it all a little more.

Don't forget that everything is seen by the

stars and that they will always

appreciate those that smile a little more

through the fire

because gratitude

is the greatest form of attitude.

Joshua Van Leader

If you lose yourself

it is not love, it is self deception

it's lethally poisonous

to self destruction

and it is why

people believe love to be blind.

somewhere between the sand and the stardust II

Some of the best memories

you may ever have

do not have to be with people.

Joshua Van Leader

Art will *Always* be necessary

for the madness must *Always* be captured.

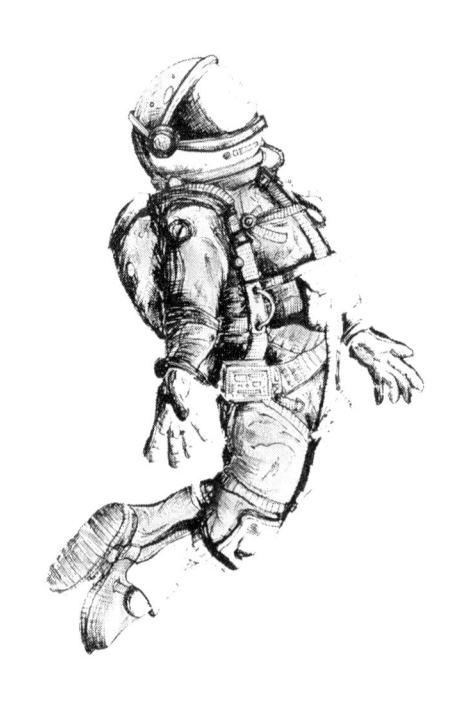

somewhere between the sand and the stardust II

Indulge in your dreams further.

So long as they believe in icons, royal blood

and other non sense,

I believe in dragons and wizards

and assuredly all our dreams.

Joshua Van Leader

Some days

I want to be left

alone

and some days

I want to stay up

and talk

about everything

under the

diamonds in the sky,

somedays I am a butterfly,

somedays, a caterpillar.

somewhere between the sand and the stardust II

It is true what they say about me.

I am miserable at times, I have been known to

be dark and upset and I am an ocean of

mystery to many, a wolf of the night. I am

misunderstood, but I am most certainly

compelled to love everything

that I do and anything I see worthy.

That's why I have a

shield and damn do I use it,

the world isn't so soft and delightful as I wish

it was, but that makes for an interesting battle.

So you see, maybe that is why they speak ill of

me, because I am in love with everything,

that you wouldn't believe in.

Joshua Van Leader

The sky is white with blue shades

covering the sky, with hits of pink

in the clouds, kissed purely by the red roar

of the sun, and there are birds flying

and fleeting across the valley,

it is riveting for my eyes to capture.

Colours bursting

forward that I only ever thought

possible in my own mind

and I am reminded again

to relax,

and to breathe

to smile inside

for my spring is here,

and I feel more alive again.

somewhere between the sand and the stardust II

You taught me a lesson

that even my happiest moments

can be

a fragmented lie.

Joshua Van Leader

Beauty and intelligence

is often a parallel poem.

somewhere between the sand and the stardust II

Pointing out

others imperfections

or correcting them

in public

doesn't make you

more intelligent, diligent or respectful,

it only confirms you are an arsehole.

Choose life.

Be fearless, proud of your scars,

be honoured if you feel a little damaged,

anyone who claims they are normal,

who claims to be untouched

not stricken by heartache

or damaged from their past,

is either a fool

or a liar

but in most cases

probably both.

somewhere between the sand and the stardust II

Continue to exercise great conviction

into your exciting, innovative, new ideas.

It is ok to fall in love with things

that most people do not,

we're all damned if

we think the same.

Joshua Van Leader

The truth is

if you don't fall in love

whether that be with

a person, a book or a passion

then you have wasted your time.

somewhere between the sand and the stardust II

Let us not forget

that as charming

and alluring

as the sky may seem.

It is the reason

for the rain, the snow, tornadoes and thunder.

Nothing is ever as pretty

and as perfect as it looks.

Joshua Van Leader

Romance is kissing

in the pouring rain

after a wild argument,

it is staying true

to what you have said

long after the feeling

you said it in

has left you.

It is staying together when things get

a little worse for wear,

it is not in a new handbag or a car,

or the next available, convenient match

that satisfies your desires

and because it's so precious and beautiful

you should *never* abuse it.

somewhere between the sand and the stardust II

All you need to create

something wonderful and unforgettable

is to fall in love,

for love

is the essence and enigma of life.

Joshua Van Leader

Art is for anyone

who wishes to feel

and we all feel.

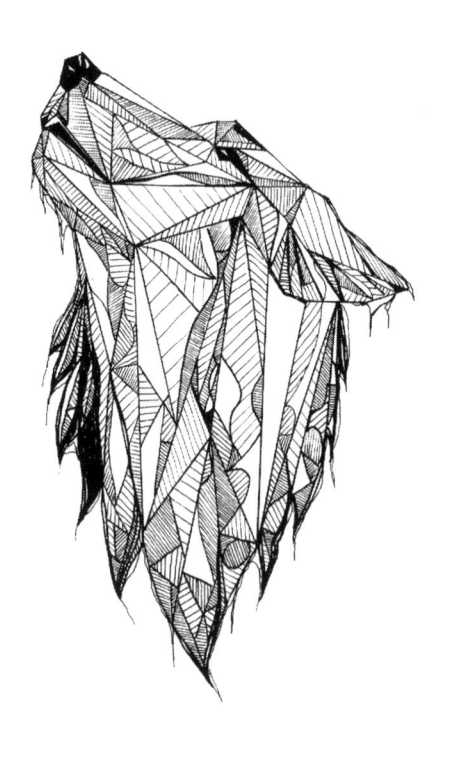

Try to admire the beauty

that is around you

rather than

just pointing out

the imperfections

and see how

your state of mind

gradually changes.

Joshua Van Leader

        To sleep next to you

    is to dream alongside you,

           I couldn't think

        of anything more

              rewarding

        or so wonderful,

         a poem in itself.

somewhere between the sand and the stardust II

You were not made to live in the shadows,

you were made

to inspire people through them.

Joshua Van Leader

You say you like diamonds

but you rarely look up at night

there is a sky full of them

and the best thing about them

is that no one

can ever take them from you.

somewhere between the sand and the stardust II

You ruined me,

but it was just the shell you destroyed,

that is all you ever touched. Even so;

I tortured my own heart and flooded my mind

with the idea of us. Drenching myself

in self pity, with my spirit overwhelmed

and the fixation that we were right

for one another. Then after time and space,

these oceans settled, I realised

it was nothing of what I truly

am and what I have to give.

That shell was torched and left behind,

now I breathe fires, as the ashes fell and went

with the trail of the wind

and what was left to build with;

was gold, pure, solid, fucking gold.

Joshua Van Leader

Chapters of Becoming -

The winter is a tale

of stillness and endurance,

the spring is a story

of flourishing, blossoming and becoming,

and the summer

is your cue to be free, fierce and wild,

then the fall,

is a reminder to shed,

to be calm and let things go.

Art should continually

be intended to be raw and rigorous,

its purpose is never to be so refined,

polished and well presented all the time.

It is a depiction of someones life,

a part of someones soul,

there has to be a chaos and a vibrance to it,

with pain and struggle, maybe.

A battle of some kind.

That sort of beauty

should never be hidden intentionally.

Joshua Van Leader

Poetry has little to do with beautiful words.

It is laughing with you,

falling asleep with you,

waking up with you,

lying in bed with you,

it is arguing with you

and then making up with you,

it is crying with you,

it is looking after you when you feel unwell,

it is travelling with you.

Poetry,

is everything

and anything

to do *with you.*

Like physics and chemistry

respect and love

are cognate.

They are interconnected.

Without one,

the other doesn't exist.

Joshua Van Leader

I lost track of the days

in fact,

the days seemed to roll into nights,

captivating my own mind that had become

engulfed into a bottomless pit

and what is anyone to do?

With uncontrollable anxiety

pressing like a torture that cannot be seen

and the worst of it,

is that because it is in the mind

it allows the disease to be easily disguised

but you can only camouflage depression

for so long

before the skies *explode*

and the seas of your mind *rupture*.

somewhere between the sand and the stardust II

It hurts.

Even though

you gave them everything you could

it wasn't enough

but it will be

for someone

who looks at the sky

the way you do,

soon

someone will look at you that way too

and you'll realise

you are

somebody's sky.

Joshua Van Leader

You can make jokes about another persons art

you can be sarcastic

about how they express themselves

but that only proves your lack of intelligence,

you're not a comedian

you're a fucking fool.

somewhere between the sand and the stardust II

Rushing is vulgar

the quicker you fall in love,

you fall out of it just the same.

Joshua Van Leader

Why did you leave?

The rain hammered down against the roof,

without you

I felt every drop,

I was drenched and soaked

in rejection, seclusion and isolation.

somewhere between the sand and the stardust II

The way they looked at one another,

    you heard the waves crash,

        you felt their souls match

            you saw the lightning flash.

But it was never as predictable as this.

You can't predict a storm like theirs.

Joshua Van Leader

So long as there is a night sky

I will dream of you.

somewhere between the sand and the stardust II

Society has

allowed

the devils

to wear

pretty faces

and the

angels are

left in scars.

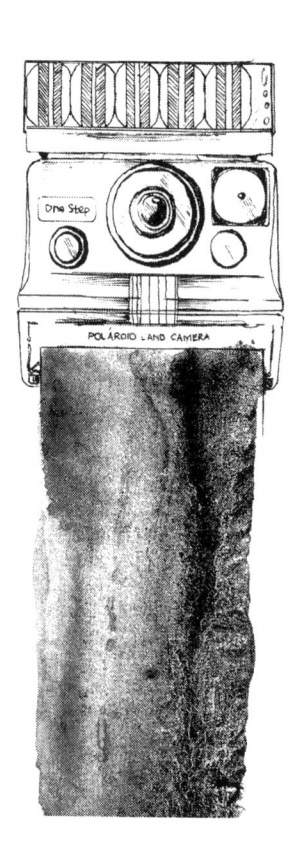

Joshua Van Leader

Well, there was nothing poetic about it,

you blinded them

flooded their thoughts

in self doubt,

split their heart

into a billion fragments of stardust.

you ripped

their fucking heart out.

somewhere between the sand and the stardust II

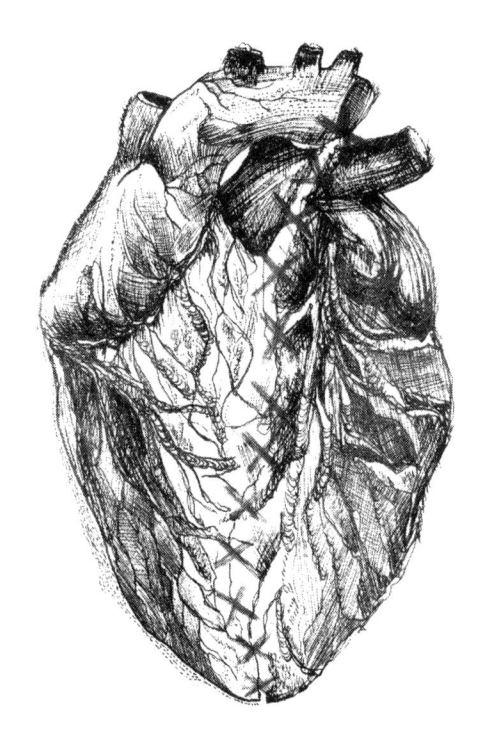

How will you feel when that supernova

reaches you?

Joshua Van Leader

Selfishness is a factor

to self destruction

not self preservation.

somewhere between the sand and the stardust II

The Stardust

A

quarter

and

a

half

of

Stardust

saudade

(n)

1. A nostalgic longing to be near again to something or someone that is distant, or that has been loved and the lost;

"the love that remains".

somewhere between the sand and the stardust II

I'm not going to tell you

how to heal, because everyones fight is unique

self enlightenment

will come from

stability of the mind and a practiced routine

of peace and balance for you to move on.

You will have to battle a pain

nobody else knows of

but that personal pain

will become your personal gain,

and it may be constantly with you

but that only means

you will be constantly stronger.

"I love you."

"I love you." He emphasised.

He said it once so she would hear it

and the second so she could feel it.

He said 'I love you."

without ever uttering a word.

It was his eyes you see,

the way he looked at her said everything

and the way

he held her close

and kissed those lips said forever.

Joshua Van Leader

You are brighter to me than anything.

You will forever

be a lighthouse to my heart

you will always

have a home

so long as I breathe.

somewhere between the sand and the stardust II

I fall in love

with you more

and more

for the way you love things

even if they don't look pretty.

You will *Always* find a way to find something

beautiful within it

and I just think

that is the most beautiful trait to have.

Joshua Van Leader

You will heal in time

but if you rush

to get out of feeling the pain

it will only ever return

and it will repeat.

Feel it, use it, forgive it

and move on at your own pace of healing.

somewhere between the sand and the stardust II

The stars only came

out to see her

dance.

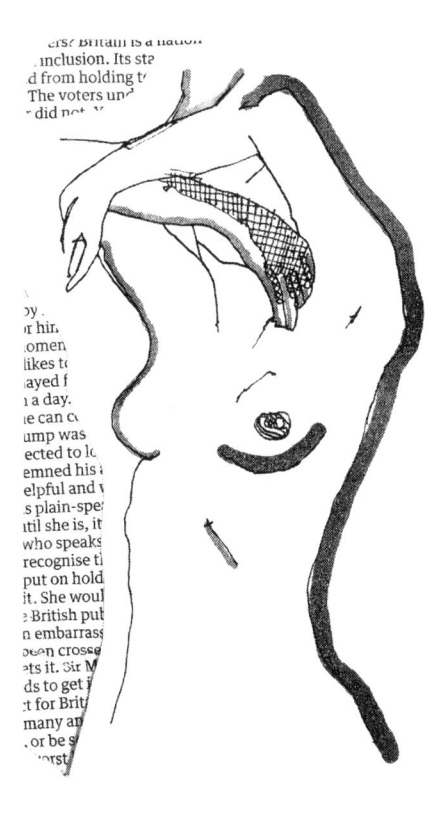

Joshua Van Leader

I think the only way to

explain it

was;

exhilarating.

Kissing you in the pouring rain,

with the echoes of thunder in the distance

it felt like kissing winter

with the warm essence of summer

in the crispness of spring.

somewhere between the sand and the stardust II

I want to find

new places with you,

I want to witness

the stars kiss the ocean

with the sand in between my toes

feeling like home once more.

I want to do it all with you

again and again and again

until it rains stardust over us.

Joshua Van Leader

The moment was enough.

I remember the stars in your eyes

when our worlds met

and waves from within us collided

tornados of blood pumping around

and hurricanes of comets inside

exploded everywhere.

The stardust settled

but only ever for a moment

and the between

will forever be

nothing

but a finger touch away.

somewhere between the sand and the stardust II

If it just feels

like another flame

then let it go

life is too short and precious

you deserve the god damn fire.

Joshua Van Leader

I know miracles exist.

It took one

for me to get away from you

and another

to love

myself all over

again.

somewhere between the sand and the stardust II

She is kissed

all over

by the stars

on her face.

She is smothered

by the universe

throughout her veins.

The galaxies

spread vast

between her fingertips

and you'll feel it,

if you ever

meet her lips.

Joshua Van Leader

I rarely admit,

but I promise;

a thousand showers

of kisses

and millions

of stars

across the sky

will be blankets to our eyes

and you will feel nothing

but treasured in

infinite comfort

when I tell you:

"I love you, I love you, I love you."

somewhere between the sand and the stardust II

There will never

be another night

like tonight,

not the way

the stars

look on you.

Joshua Van Leader

Only when writing does love

have anything to do with

the heart,

other than that

it's all in your fucking head,

so if you think

you are going crazy,

then shit,

you probably are.

somewhere between the sand and the stardust II

Often it is the truth that hurts.

But it is the secrets we keep that destroy us.

Joshua Van Leader

She didn't enjoy poetry

she couldn't seem resonate it.

How he wrote such well strung sentences

and interesting words felt unnatural.

Slowly she digested it,

gaining an insight

they would speak

as they wandered

the fields, the beaches, the streets.

Taking in the night sky,

she became more articulate

grasping;

everything was poetry

herself

unquestionably included.

somewhere between the sand and the stardust II

The secret is that

that there is no secret.

We are all chasing a happiness.

A void

that is not sustainable and practical,

stop wanting things so fast

and step back into nature

into yourself

slow down

and

Breathe.

Joshua Van Leader

As the rain fell lightly

the trees danced

among the music of the wind

the birds joined me in my melancholy

and I fell deeper in love with you.

It was as poetic as it was tragically natural.

somewhere between the sand and the stardust II

You are my night sky

my moon,

the stars, you are everything calm.

You are everything safe in the night

everyone takes such elegance,

such magic, such beauty

for granted.

I will never be used

to looking at you.

Your love channeled me to love myself more

and I forever love and thank you for that.

That is all I ever needed.

To feel loved, again.

somewhere between the sand and the stardust II

He met her

and that was that

love transformed him,

it was the most beautiful thing

I have ever seen

and the most beautiful thing

he had ever felt.

Joshua Van Leader

Please give me some time,

I am still reminded of you

whenever it rains hard,

or when the stars aglow

I am still taken to that night

that felt as if it were scripted

it was too perfect for me.

I wanted it to be you

I still do

oh damn,

I really did.

oh damn.

I really do.

somewhere between the sand and the stardust II

Your words have never left me

not even

after all this time.

I'm starting to to believe

they will stain my skin

like the stars decorate and glisten in the night.

Joshua Van Leader

No matter what you believe

yourself to be,

you are loved

you carry

something very special

in your core

I know because

I am one of those that reveres you,

you helped heal me

without you even knowing it.

somewhere between the sand and the stardust II

I imagined a future with you

sadly, that is all that it will ever be.

An imaginative, romanticised idea

of you and I,

we are not compatible.

I watch the stars most nights in awe

and you forget they even exist

where I see beauty and magic

you just see the sky.

Joshua Van Leader

These are not tears for you

they are your lies

leaking out of me

so I can let you go

and not have to carry anything more

to do with you.

somewhere between the sand and the stardust II

I've always believed

I cry salt water.

The tears you see

will dry up

reassembling

into stardust.

This magic you see

is always worth

a little hurt sometimes.

"Look at the sky this evening,

look at how beautiful it is."

"No, thank you."

He replied

"I'll just keep looking at you."

somewhere between the sand and the stardust II

I remember street lights

everything seemed to intertwine.

I just kissed you

and it stained my soul

everything else became a blur.

Joshua Van Leader

I forget we are from the same place

you and I

you have a mind

drenched in riches of another world.

Still, I feel at home

as I ever have

and I ever will with anyone,

perfectly; you are my home.

somewhere between the sand and the stardust II

In all the poetry that I read

I find versions of you in every one

and I see us in every line.

Joshua Van Leader

I'd like to believe what brought me to you

were from the stars above

something magical and mysterious

but it wasn't.

It was whiskey,

a few poems

and a heartbreak here or there.

somewhere between the sand and the stardust II

Joshua Van Leader

I'm struggling to be whole

striving to centre myself

to focus on where it went wrong.

You took part of me with you

when you left

I would wait

for the sun to come up every morning

with good news

that you will return this missing piece.

The truth is;

you are a tyrant of love,

somewhere between the sand and the stardust II

you are ignorant to my dignity

propriety doesn't even enter your thoughts

so why have I waited for part of me to return

with a chance of you with it.

Well you can have it,

it is worthless now

I am building a new fragment,

a blazing remnant

a fierce and electric element,

something that you can't touch,

not because it's out of reach but

because you cant fathom a brilliance like that.

Joshua Van Leader

The way you have

loved me

all these years

is the reason why

I believe

you

to be the greatest artist I know.

somewhere between the sand and the stardust II

"It is love

and the idea of it

the idea of not being good enough

that makes me

hate myself."

"Well then my dear,

it is not love at all."

Joshua Van Leader

I will hold your hand

when you are blind

I will remind you of your wings

when you forget you can fly

I will be there when everything around you

is f a
    l l i
        n g

.

somewhere between the sand and the stardust II

When I am with her,

I find the shadows are chasing us

struggling to keep up,

the sky is on fire

the sea is drowning

all the stardust inside us;

screaming out

jump, love, kiss, give

and live

in this forever now.

Joshua Van Leader

Loving you is

intoxicating,

it is lightweight

it is rain and snow

it is spring

and blooming flowers and calm seas

and magnificent sunsets.

It is everything.

You are the essence for my strength

and you are the seed to my inspiration.

Joshua Van Leader

"Where to?"

He said.

"To a golden place

where it bursts

everyday

with magic and wondrous colours

and even when it rains

it's warm."

"You're already there."

He replied,

"Just look within."

somewhere between the sand and the stardust II

When it comes to love

second chances

should be as rare as snow in summer.

Joshua Van Leader

It had next to nothing

to do with the way you looked

it was everything

that we could talk about

how we effortlessly made one another

feel almost infinite,

like we were on fire

like we could fly, touch the stars

we were in love for all the right reasons

they were reasons

that I never knew existed.

The moonlight

shimmered through the windows,

the silhouette of the flowers

he brought earlier,

remain shaped on the wall

with the help of the candles flicker.

In the background

the sound of violins and cellos

could be heard from a few streets over

with the soft thin air summer held,

everything seemed content and full

of busting life, he had an idea

of what luxury truly was.

Questioning; *"Is this perfection?*

Is this what people mean

when they talk of a moment stopped in time,

was it as good as it could ever be?"

Joshua Van Leader

Tell her, when you can:

"You have been the ocean air to my character.

A hurricane in phases,

bringing the calm humidity

that succeeds it,

you have been fire, raging fire

with a flamboyant elegance

of that neighboured to a sunset.

You have paused me

several times when I needed it

I have found myself

thinking of you;

somewhere between the sand and the stardust II

thoughts of a future perhaps

and you are always the first thing

to come to me when I look at the stars.

It is never that I need you

only life is a little more pleasant with you,

knowing you are untroubled and safe

I hope, one day I can repay your favour

in offering you my undivided love

and affection

one day perhaps,

maybe even make you aware

of your magical charismatic touch

held at your very fingertips.

Joshua Van Leader

I am reminded of you everywhere

and I don't feel the cold

in the air anymore

I just feel

the burning of your absence

and the empty promises

linger like ash

around me.

somewhere between the sand and the stardust II

I do believe in destiny

as I have looked at the stars

many times

and felt nothing

then

after I met you,

the stars

never quite

felt the same again.

Joshua Van Leader

When I fell for you,

it felt like I fell from the skies,

and I am still falling now,

or am I flying?

I can't tell the difference.

somewhere between the sand and the stardust II

The moment their lips touched

reminded him

the first time he felt the rain

and reminded her

the first time she saw the stars.

Joshua Van Leader

"I am not sure if

I am ready to fall in love.

I am very sure it is you though"

"I don't have time to wait around,

I have places to be, and a world to see

I will tell you now;

this is as greater time as any,

just give me a worthy devotion

with sincere actions,

committed words and honest eyes,

and we'll figure the rest out as we go."

somewhere between the sand and the stardust II

"I cant really remember."

What a lie.

Joshua Van Leader

He remembered everything

his heart raced

like never before.

His life felt built up for just

those moments with the palms of his hands

getting clammy of the nervous kind.

He felt eruptions inside,

his thoughts were lost in time

out of tune from his mind

he became stagnant and

charm evaporated away

from his fingertips,

he fell in love alright

and he remembers every second of it

in the blink of an eyelid,

he fell in love

and there was little anything or anyone

could ever do to prevent it.

somewhere between the sand and the stardust II

The only analogy

I could think to describe you

is: ***the ocean.***

Joshua Van Leader

They did everything together

but *grow*.

That is the root for all the other 'reasons',

people do not make it through together.

somewhere between the sand and the stardust II

All I ask

is you break me gently next time.

Joshua Van Leader

Lets talk? -

Sure, we can talk about

how our love was unfinished

maybe we deserved a little longer together.

We can also talk about

how your lack of dignity and respect for me

was insulting and rather disgraceful too?

Now, watch me <u>rise</u>.

Were you expecting that?

somewhere between the sand and the stardust II

I was falling in love

and falling

apart

and I couldn't tell the difference.

Joshua Van Leader

Live by the sea

with me

and under the scattered skies;

love me.

somewhere between the sand and the stardust II

All I want is

to see you blossom like spring,

rise like the summer sun

find comfort in living.

You are not just a person to me

you are art

a poem

a galaxy of inspiration

a gaseous nebula of boundless love.

You are to me

what the salt is to the sea

and what the sun is to the moon;

a defying parallel

of the other

hopelessly connected, by destiny,

by love, by science,

or maybe by pure chance.

Joshua Van Leader

I closed my eyes

instead of seeing darkness

I saw you and stars and

my favourite colours.

I realised then

we were more than best friends,

I realised then you take me to another place

no one else can

and that I love you

quite a little more than what I have said.

somewhere between the sand and the stardust II

Nothing has ever felt so galvanic,

and I have never felt so alive

then being in love with you.

Joshua Van Leader

You are the perfect balance for someone

continue to bloom.

Someone,

somewhere

has waited their life to find you

and to spend a lifetime with you.

somewhere between the sand and the stardust II

Let it go

one star said

heal

said another.

Find forgiveness from the centre

said a distant star.

Lastly,

the moon leaned in and whispered

be brave, you are deserving

of all beautiful things

love will find you again.

Joshua Van Leader

You are not like anyone else

to me

I see you with crystals

and diamonds in your eyes

even oceans, swirling fires

thunderstorms and lightning too.

somewhere between the sand and the stardust II

He watches the stars each night,

wanders out

into the ocean of blackness.

He just sits

among them upstairs

looking for her,

he just never gives up.

Joshua Van Leader

You maybe having a bad day

but you make my day brighter

by just being next to me,

I have never known a happiness like this.

somewhere between the sand and the stardust II

There isn't anyone that gets me like you do

and I'm glad

because I don't want anyone else.

Joshua Van Leader

I can't live in halves.

I don't know much about maybes.

My do's and my do nots are staple clear

and I'm all in

I'm all yours.

somewhere between the sand and the stardust II

I wonder if

we will still look at the stars

the same way we do now

when we're older;

extensively with wonder

holding hands,

and a little drunk

with dreams that match

the idea that we are enough.

Joshua Van Leader

To Love

Remember that you are

an accumulation

of beautiful moments and decisions,

you are worthy of the most powerful

emotion ever known to us

and you can give it too

which makes you in return

an incredibly powerful person.

somewhere between the sand and the stardust II

Joshua Van Leader

somewhere between the sand and the stardust II

Joshua Van Leader

Warmest & Greatest

Thanks -

somewhere between the sand and the stardust II

To my parents

for supporting my difficult path,

for their abiding love,

permanent support and lasting confidence

in myself and my creative subjects.

Together we have endured

a substantial amount of pain

and I am deeply inspired by you.

To you all who purchased one of my books,

or supported my other art forms.

I am profoundly grateful.

To all the health organisations that have aided

to my recovery and eased

my pain in order for me to rise

with strength and purpose.

Joshua Van Leader

About the Author

Joshua Van Leader is an English painter, fashion designer and writer. He lives better by the sea or talking to the stars.

For more information on following the adventure follow these links below:

www.joshuavanleader.com

instagram.com/joshuavanleader

Joshua Van Leader

somewhere between the sand and the stardust II

Printed in Poland
by Amazon Fulfillment
Poland Sp. z o.o., Wrocław